CRYSTAL UNICORNS

ANNUAL 2022

CRYSTAL UNICORNS ANNUAL 2022
A LAUGHING LOBSTER BOOK 978-1-913906-72-6
Published in Great Britain by Laughing Lobster an imprint of Centum Publishing Ltd.
This edition published 2021.
1 3 5 7 9 10 8 6 4 2

© 2021 Laughing Lobster an imprint of Centum Publishing Ltd. All Rights Reserved.

Illustrations by Charlotte Archer.

No part of this publication may be reproduced, stored in a retrieval system, or
transmitted in any form or by any means, electronic, mechanical, photocopying,
recording or otherwise, without the prior permission of the publishers.

Laughing Lobster an imprint of Centum Publishing Ltd, 20 Devon Square,
Newton Abbot, Devon, TQ12 2HR, UK
9/10 Fenian St, Dublin 2, D02 RX24 Ireland

books@centumpublishingltd.co.uk

LAUGHING LOBSTER AN IMPRINT OF
CENTUM PUBLISHING LIMITED. Reg. No. 08497203

A CIP catalogue record for this book is available
from the British Library.

Printed in China.

WELCOME

Come join the enchanting unicorns in this magical book.

hello

Turn to pages 6, 16, 24 and 54 to get to know the unicorns and their friends.

There are lots of cute crafts to make in this UNICORN-TASTIC book.

Check out the doorhanger on page 43, create your own unicorn model on page 45 and a code wheel for you and your bestie on page 47.

Cute alert!

SHHH!
DO NOT DISTURB!
UNICORN DREAMS
IN PROGRESS

UNICORN FRIENDS

Grab your colours and transform these friends with all the colours of the rainbow.

30

Add a rainbow of colours to all the creative colouring pages inside.

Get your brain in gear with all the magical puzzles inside, from mazes to lots to spot!

SKATE PARK

Help this lost unicorn skate her way through the maze to find her friend.

START

FINISH

58

WHICH WAY?

Which path should these baby unicorns take to reach Crystal Unicorn?

Which path will lead them to ice creams?

Which path will lead them to the rain cloud?

READY PLAYER ONE?

Zoom to page 32 to create your own unicorn game or check out if you can keep a secret on page 56.

You can find all the answers for the puzzles at the back of the book.

MEET THE UNICORNS

Discover lots of fun facts about Crystal Unicorn and her friends.

CRYSTAL UNICORN

LIVES IN: Crystal Castle

LIKES: crystals, gems, jewels and flying

Can you give Crystal Unicorn a makeover by transforming her colours so she looks different?

Yum yum!

GEM AND JEWEL UNICORN
(TWINS)

LIVE IN: Crystal Castle

LIKE: playing games, puzzles and ice cream

DAISY UNICORN

LIVES IN: Crystal Castle

LIKES: flowers, woods and exploring

GO EXPLORING

Follow the clues below to work out which friends are exploring where. When you find their location, write their initials on the map.

Spot Crystal Unicorn.

- Head east 2 squares.
- Go north 5 squares.
- Turn west 1 square.

Find Rainbow Unicorn.

- Go north 4 squares.
- Head west 1 square.
- Drop south 2 squares.

Race to it and track Moonbeam Unicorn.

- Head north 6 squares.
- Turn east 2 squares.
- Go south 3 squares.

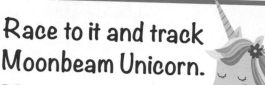

Where is Filbert Frog?

- Move north 2 squares.
- Go east 2 squares.
- Head north 2 squares.

Now write some instructions to explain how to find Sparkle Unicorn.

Find Loveheart Unicorn!

- Head north 4 squares.
- Go east 1 square.
- Move south 3 squares.

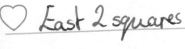

♡ North 5 squares

♡ East 2 squares

♡

N
W · E
S

CU FF

MU

BU

UU

START

9

RAINBOW SPOTTER

Can you spot 10 differences between the pictures below?

RAINBOW WATERFALL

Add every colour of the rainbow to the picture below.

UNICORN MAKEOVER

Grab your pens and transform these unicorns with lots of sparkling colours.

UNICORN CREATIONS

Trace over the lines and add some colour to finish off the unicorn friends.

HELLO TEAM UNICORN

Discover what makes each of these friendly unicorns unique.

SHIMMER UNICORN

LIVES IN: Unicorn Castle

LIKES: parties, cupcakes, presents and balloons

MOONBEAM UNICORN

LIVES IN: Unicorn Castle

LIKES: daydreaming, a full moon and sleeping

JIGSAW JUMBLE

Can you work out which pieces go where
to complete the picture of the unicorn meadow?

INTO THE WOODS

Colour by numbers and follow the colour key to transform these unicorns.

19

MATCH UP!

Can you help Gem and Jewel draw lines between these objects to match them into pairs?

PICTURE PERFECT

Can you match the correct caption to the right picture?

④ A

B ③

③ C

D ①

22

E

F

G

1. We ♥ skateboarding!

2. Wish you were here?

3. BLAST OFF!

4. Is it a bird, is it a plane? No, it's SUPER UNICORN!

5. #parklife

6. Why fly when you can swim!

7. Shimmy, shake, boogie on down!

23

SAY HI TO THE UNICORNS

These sparkly, shimmery unicorns love to dance and prance with their friends.

STARDUST UNICORN

LIVES IN: Crystal Castle

LIKES: stars, flying, crystals and exploring

All you need is love and unicorns.

LOVEHEART UNICORN

LIVES IN: Crystal Castle

LIKES: climbing, flying, swimming and exploring

STARLIGHT UNICORN

LIVES IN: Unicorn Castle

LIKES: shooting stars, midnight feasts and dancing

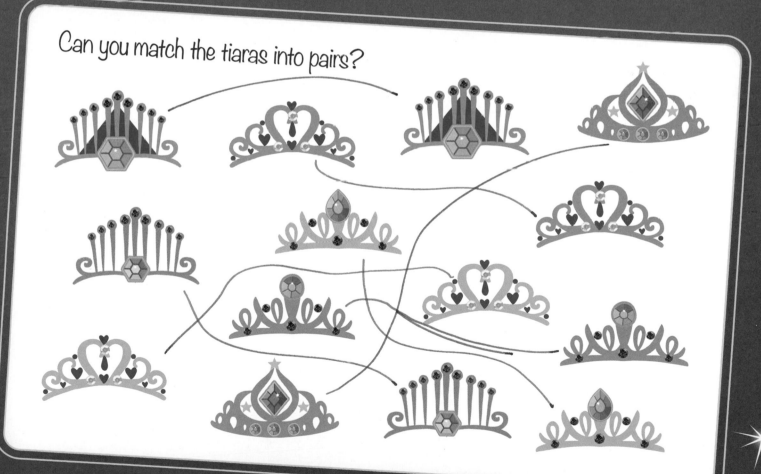

Can you match the tiaras into pairs?

SNOWBALL FUN

Draw some unicorns, doodle
some snowballs and add some
colour to finish off this snowy scene.

BFF

Everything is better with friends by your side! Who's your BFF?

Draw or stick in pictures of you and your best friend in the frames below, and then fill in the BFF bio.

My BFF's name is **Oscar**

They are **17** years old

We have been BFFs since **November 2020**

Their favourite food is **Steak**

Their favourite hobby is **Being with me**

28

Fill in this page
with your bestie.

My fave thing about my BFF is
His adorableness

My BFF's favourite
thing about me is
My amazing personality

Our fave thing to do together is
Cuddle

We are different because
He is smart

We are the same because
We are both nerds

We will be friends forever and
always because I love
him lots and bts
and he loves me too,
we really get along
and he is patient
with me which
means we don't
get into many
fights.

ME		MY BFF
Not choosing	KITTENS OR PUPPIES?	idk
sweets	CUPCAKES OR SWEETS?	sweets
chocolate	CHOCOLATE OR CRISPS?	chocolate
both & boogy	DANCING OR SINGING?	neither
sport	READING OR SPORT?	both
art	ART OR CRAFTS?	neither
snow	SNOW OR SUNSHINE?	sun
TV	TV OR MOVIES?	TV

UNICORN FRIENDS

Grab your colours and transform these friends with all the colours of the rainbow.

GAME ON

Use this space to create your own unicorn gaming adventure.

⭐ 1

Choose which characters you would like in your game.

○ Sparkle

○ Shimmer

○ Rainbow

○ Moonbeam

○ Starlight

○ Crystal

○ Daisy

○ Loveheart

○ Stardust

○ Gem and Jewel

⭐ 2

Next, choose a setting for your game.

○ Rainbow Waterfall

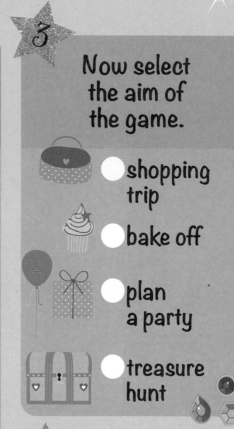

○ Crystal Castle

○ Unicorn Woods

○ Crystal Caves

⭐ 3

Now select the aim of the game.

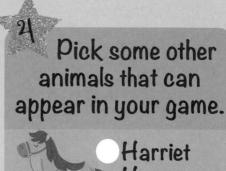

○ shopping trip

○ bake off

○ plan a party

○ treasure hunt

⭐ 4

Pick some other animals that can appear in your game.

○ Harriet Horse

○ Lili Ladybird

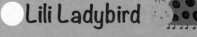

○ Fluttershy Butterfly

○ Filbert Frog

○ Chirpy Chick

5 Tick a picture to show what the weather is like, during your game.

 ○ sunny

 ○ cloudy

 ○ rainbow

 ○ rainy

○ snowy

Use these spaces to create some scenes from your game, as they might appear on screen.

READY PLAYER ONE?

WHERE AM I?

Can you help Gem work out where Jewel is playing, using her clues?

A4

RAINBOW WATERFALL

C3

CRYSTAL CAVES

sB

OVER THE RAINBOW

2 There are lots and lots of tall trees and the grass has turned purple.

1 Oooh, I'm chilly, it's cold here but the sky looks magical.

3 Everything is light and sparkly here, even though I am inside.

D₂ UNICORN WOODS

F₁ CRYSTAL CASTLE

E₆ UNICORN CASTLE

5
Wee-heeeee! I am flying high above a rainbow in lots of fluffy clouds.

6
There is so much space here to gallop and afterwards I'm off to the castle for cake.

4
Splish splash.... I love to chill out here. It's so cool and the noise of the flowing water is wonderful.

HIDE & SEEK

Can you spot 10 unicorns hiding in the woods?

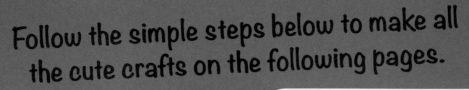

MAKE IT!

Follow the simple steps below to make all the cute crafts on the following pages.

NOTELETS
pages 39 to 42

Cut out the sweet notelets from pages 39 to 42, fill them in and give them to your friends and family.

UNICORN FRIEND
page 45

- Colour in the unicorn tail, horn, ears and mane in your own choice of colours.

- Cut around the dotted lines of the templates on page 45.

- Stick the cloud to a piece of card, to make a base.

- Stick the feet of the unicorn body to the cloud, so the body is curved.

- Roll the head piece up and stick together where it says 'glue here'.

- Attach the head to the body with glue, then glue the ears, horn and hair to the head.

- Glue both sides of the tail together and attach to the body with glue.

DOORHANGER
page 43

- Cut around the dotted lines to remove the template from pages 43 and 44.
- Fold it in half and glue together to create a super-cute doorhanger for your bedroom door.

SHHH!
DO NOT DISTURB!
UNICORN DREAMS IN PROGRESS

TO:

DREAM BIG

FROM:

UNICORN POWER

Be a unicorn

DEAR

 FROM

BELIEVE
in YOURSELF

I MAY LOOK LIKE I'M LISTENING TO YOU, BUT INSIDE MY HEAD I'M

RIDING A UNICORN.

ROLL ME IN FAIRY DUST AND CALL ME A UNICORN!

I'M A UNICORN

TEAM UNICORN

Reach 4 the STARS

ALWAYS BE YOURSELF

unless you are a unicorn (and then always be a unicorn).

ALWAYS

BFF

_____
_____
_____
_____
_____
_____
_____

DEAR _____
_____
_____
_____
_____
_____
_____
_____
_____
_____

FROM _____

Be a unicorn
in a field
of horses.

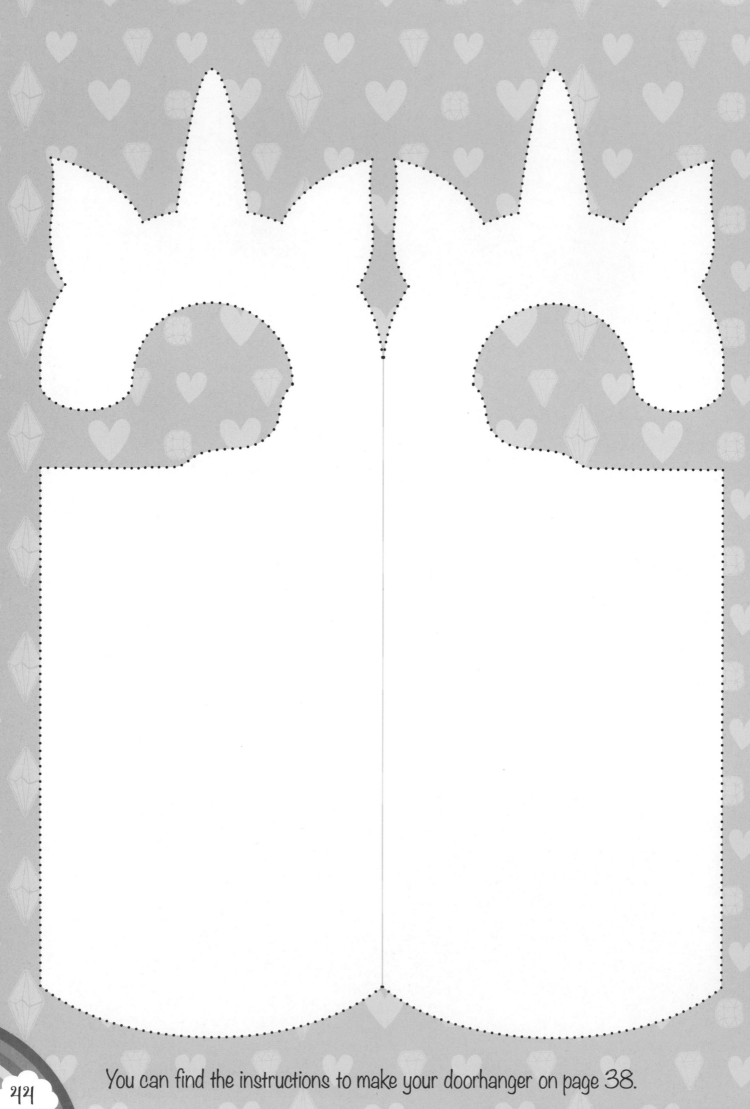

You can find the instructions to make your doorhanger on page 38.

glue here

You can find the instructions to make your unicorn friend on page 38.

SECRET NOTES

Create a cute code wheel for you and your BFF to keep your messages top secret.

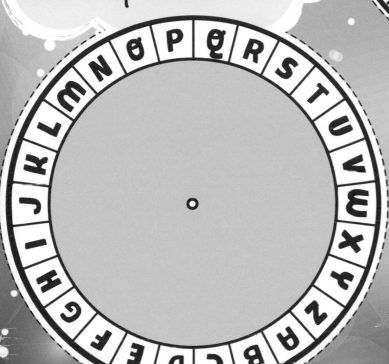

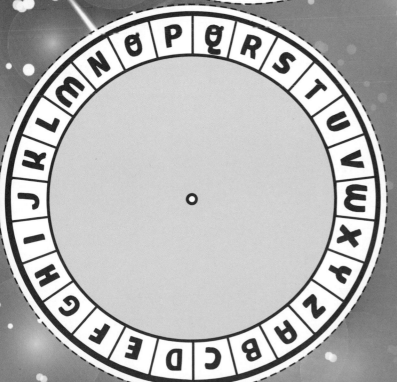

♥ 1   Cut out the big circles and the little circles.

♥ 2   Use a split pin to join a big circle with a small circle (the small circles should be placed on top of the bigger circles).

♥ 3   Spin the smaller circle to a position where the letters are incorrectly aligned.

♥ 4   Choose one pair of letters to remember your code, for example your cipher could be A = T (make sure you don't forget it).

♥ 5   Write a short sentence, encoding it using the smaller circle letters instead of the larger circle letters.

♥ 6   Give a code wheel to a friend – give her your cipher eg A = T and see if she can decode your message.

247

48

GO DOTTY!

Join the dots then transform these unicorns with your pens.

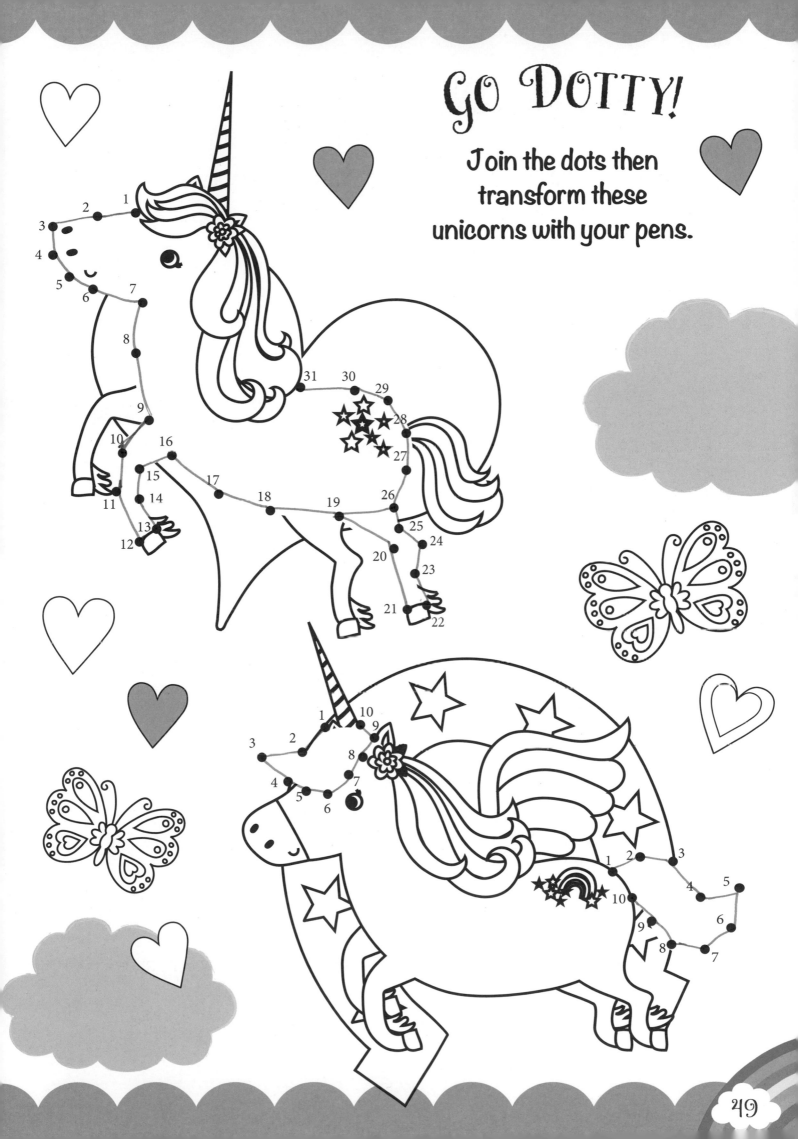

DECISION HELPER

Follow the simple steps below and use the template opposite to create your own unicorn decision helper.

 1 Cut out the template on the opposite page, then fold each corner to the opposite corner. Then open up again to create creases in your paper.

The four unicorns should now be showing.

 2 Fold all corners to the centre of the square.

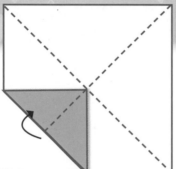

It should now look like this.

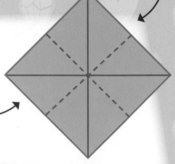

 3 Next, turn your template over so the folds are face down and fold each corner in to the centre.

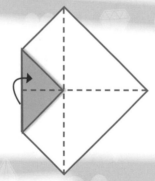

Now you should see the numbers.

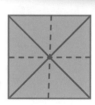

 4 Next, fold your template in half vertically and then again horizontally.

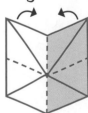
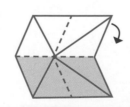

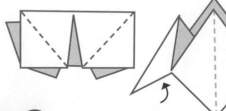

 5 Insert your fingers and thumbs underneath the flaps you have created.

50

Make sure you complete the colouring activity on the next page before you cut out the template.

HOW TO PLAY

1 Ask a question that has a yes or no answer and pick a character.

2 Open the decision helper in alternating directions, one time each for every letter of the character's name.

3 Then pick a number and open the decision helper this many times, in alternating directions.

4 Pick another number then lift that flap to reveal the answer to your question.

TRUE COLOURS

Bring this meadow to life with
your brightest colours.

SAY HI TO THE UNICORN FRIENDS

Discover lots of fun facts about these friendly animals.

Did you know that butterflies can taste with their feet?

LILI LADYBIRD

LIVES IN: the enchanted forest

LIKES: tap dancing, singing and somersaults

FLUTTERSHY BUTTERFLY

LIVES IN: the enchanted forest

LIKES: flowers, flying and playing games

Ladybirds can have spots, stripes or no markings at all.

CHIRPY CHICK

LIVES IN: the enchanted forest

LIKES: chatting, stories and visiting her friends for tea parties

BILL BUTTERFLY

LIVES IN: the enchanted forest

LIKES: flying, flowers, trees and nectar

HARRIET HORSE

LIVES IN: the enchanted forest

LIKES: sparkly gems and jewels, prancing and her unicorn friends

HA HA!
What do stylish frogs wear?
Jumpsuits.

Crooooooak!

FILBERT FROG

LIVES IN: the enchanted pond

LIKES: jumping, swimming and poking his tongue out

Add some colours to these ladybirds so each one looks different.

CAN YOU KEEP A SECRET?

Take the quiz and discover how good you are at keeping secrets.

1 How do you feel when a friend shares a secret with you?

Ⓐ I feel glad that they trust me and will promise to keep it a secret.

Ⓑ A bit worried, but will do my best to keep their secret safe.

Ⓒ I don't want to know. I hate being asked to keep secrets.

2 When a friend tells you a secret, you ...

Ⓐ Say nothing. Secrets are always safe with me.

Ⓑ I might tell my mum or another bestie, but only if they ask.

Ⓒ Tell lots of people, I am hopeless at keeping things to myself.

3 You're with your BFF when they have a really embarrassing moment. What do you do?

Ⓐ Keep it between us, that's what friends are for.

Ⓑ If it was really funny I might tell someone else, but make them promise not to share.

Ⓒ I'd just have to share it with our other BFFs, too.

4 A friend wants to share someone else's secret. What do you do?

Ⓐ Tell them to stop. I don't want to hear secrets I'm not supposed to know.

Ⓑ Let them tell me, as it might help them to share.

Ⓒ Listen carefully. Everyone likes a bit of gossip.

Hey! Can you keep a secret?

Shhh! Don't say another word!

MOSTLY A'S

You are a true super-hero secret keeper. Your friends know their secrets are always safe with you. You know the importance of keeping quiet and keeping secrets. But you also know that it is okay to tell a secret to a parent or grown-up if you think a friend might be hurt or in trouble.

MOSTLY B'S

You do really try to keep people's secrets but sometimes you just can't help letting them slip. Don't worry, this still makes you a good friend but try to do as your friends ask when they share their secrets and they will return the favour when you share yours with them.

MOSTLY C'S

You love to talk and have a gossip which means that secret keeping is not your best skill. It's okay to let your friends know if you find it hard to keep secrets under wraps. That way you're being honest with them.

SKATE PARK

Help this lost unicorn skate her way through the maze to find her friend.

START

FINISH

WHICH WAY?

Which path should Gem and Jewel take to reach Crystal Unicorn?

Which path will lead them to ice creams?

Which path will lead them to the rain cloud?

SEEK AND SPOT

Can you spot all the friends in the word grid opposite? When you do, tick them off and add some colour to complete the pictures.

○ CRYSTAL

○ LOVEHEART

○ SPARKLE

○ STARLIGHT

○ MOONBEAM

○ RAINBOW

○ STARDUST

○ DAISY

○ GEM

○ JEWEL

○ LILI

○ FILBERT

○ HARRIET

○ SHIMMER

○ BILL

○ CHIRPY

○ FLUTTERSHY

P Y V H Y N N K F B T T M L

P W G S S H A P O W E K U O

N B I L G Y F G F U I P Y V

Y A I T R E B L I F R V J E

D L B Y U C M V C Z R Q S H

I T H G I L R A T S A I M E

T V G E F S B Y E B H M Y A

J Q A W Q H A Z S G N H S R

W E K L K I M Y X T S T V T

O C W S L M H A P R A Z Y V

B N V E X M K U E R N L N R

N U Y H L E F T D B I Z O P

I W R Z Q R T U K I N H X D

A U Z G L U S B I L L O C S

R V U H L T W X Z K A W O Y

F H I F H K R I K J E K F M

S P A R K L E P X Z L Z F Q

J O S J I V X E Y T I G L Q

HIGH FLIERS

Use the colour key to colour by numbers
and give these unicorns a makeover.

63

BORN TO BE DIFFERENT!

Ever wondered what it would be like to be something completely different? What would you be?

IF I WAS A COLOUR I WOULD BE...

IF I WAS AN ANIMAL I WOULD BE A...

IF I WAS A POP STAR I WOULD BE JUST LIKE...

IF I WAS A CHOCOLATE BAR I WOULD BE A...

IF I WAS A MOVIE STAR I WOULD BE JUST LIKE...

IF I COULD LIVE IN AN ONLINE GAME I WOULD LIVE IN...

IF I WAS AN ICE-CREAM FLAVOUR I WOULD TASTE LIKE...

_____

IF I WAS A NUMBER I WOULD BE NUMBER...

_____

IF I COULD BE ANYONE IN THE WORLD I WOULD BE...

_____

IF I WAS A PLANET I WOULD BE...

_____

IF I COULD GIVE MYSELF A NEW NAME IT WOULD BE...

_____

IF I WAS A FLOWER I WOULD BE A...

_____

IF I WAS A SUPERHERO I WOULD BE...

_____

SPOT IT

The smaller pictures may all look the same as the big picture, but there is something different in each one. Can you spot what?

HIDDEN MESSAGE

Use this super stealthy way to write secret notes to your BFFs! Just follow the steps below to create some invisible ink.

WHAT YOU NEED:

- ❤ 1 bowl
- ❤ 2 cotton buds
- ❤ ¼ cup of baking soda
- ❤ ¼ cup of water
- ❤ ¼ cup of a dark coloured juice, like cranberry juice
- ❤ white paper

> Oooh, I love a secret message!

WHAT YOU DO:

1. Ask an grown-up to help you add the water and baking soda to a bowl, and carefully mix them together.
2. Dip a cotton bud into the mixture.
3. Use the cotton bud to write your message on the paper.
4. Wait until the ink is completely dry.
5. Dip the other cotton bud into the juice.
6. Paint the juice over your message and wait for it to appear – just like magic!

> Ask a grown-up to help with the tricky bits.

ODD ONE OUT

Can you spot the odd unicorn out in each row?

1 A B C D E

2 A B C D

3 A B C D E F

4 A B C D

5 A B C D E F

6 A B C D E

FLY HIGH

Go dot to dot to finish
off the castle then colour
in all the unicorns
on the page.

PLAY TIME

Check out these fun games to play with your friends.

GO TEAM UNICORN

INSTRUCTIONS:

- choose one player to go off and hide
- the rest of the players must seek them out
- when they find them, they must sqaush into the hiding place with them
- the last person to find them becomes the hider for the next game

Treasure HUNTERS

INSTRUCTIONS:

- Gather together around 10 items of treasure - these could be anything, for example, coins, biscuits, socks, hair bobbles etc
- ask all the players to close their eyes, while you hide all the treasure items - you could hide them in a room, or around a house or garden
- the players then have five minutes to find all the treasure, the player who finds the most items, wins

WHO AM I?

INSTRUCTIONS:

- fill a bowl with sticky notes with names written on them - these could be names of friends, teachers, sports stars, historical figures or movie actors
- each person takes a note, then sticks it to the forehead of the person next to them, so that everyone has a note on their head and everyone else can read it
- take it in turns to guess who you are by asking your friends a yes or no question
- the player to guess correctly first, wins

MEMORY MUDDLE

Stare at this picture for 30 seconds and try to remember as many things about it as you can. Then turn the page and try to answer the questions.

See how much you can remember about the picture on the previous page and answer the questions below.

1. Who is crossing the bridge?
A Crystal Unicorn
B Harriet Horse
C Filbert Frog

2. How many trees did you spot in the picture?
A one
B two
C three

3. What is growing on the grass?
A carrots
B gems
C flowers

4. Who is splashing about in the stream?
A Jewel and Gem Unicorns
B Fluttershy and Bill Butterfly
C Nobody

5. What is Crystal Unicorn collecting?
A sparkly crystals
B sparkly stars
C sparkly coins

6. Who isn't in the picture?
A Loveheart Unicorn
B Chirpy Chick
C Lili Ladybird

CREATE YOUR OWN UNICORN

What colour would it be?

○ ♥ ○ ♥ ○
○ ♥ ○ ♥ ○

What symbol would it have?

Tick 3 special skills you would give it.	○ super speed	○ breathe underwater	○ night vision
	○ invisibility	○ super strength	○ magical horn

Draw your unicorn here. ⤵

_____ _____

Give your unicorn a name. Its first name could be the season you were born in.

Followed by either the last thing you ate or your favourite colour.

DOTTY FUN

Find a friend and challenge them to this fun game.

1 Take it in turns to draw a vertical or horizontal line between each dot.

2 Each time you complete a box, mark your initials inside it.

3 An empty box is worth 1 point, a gem box is worth 2 points, a heart box is worth 3 points, a rainbow box is worth 4 points and a unicorn box is worth 5 points.

4 When all the dots have been joined up, add up your scores. The player with the most points, wins.

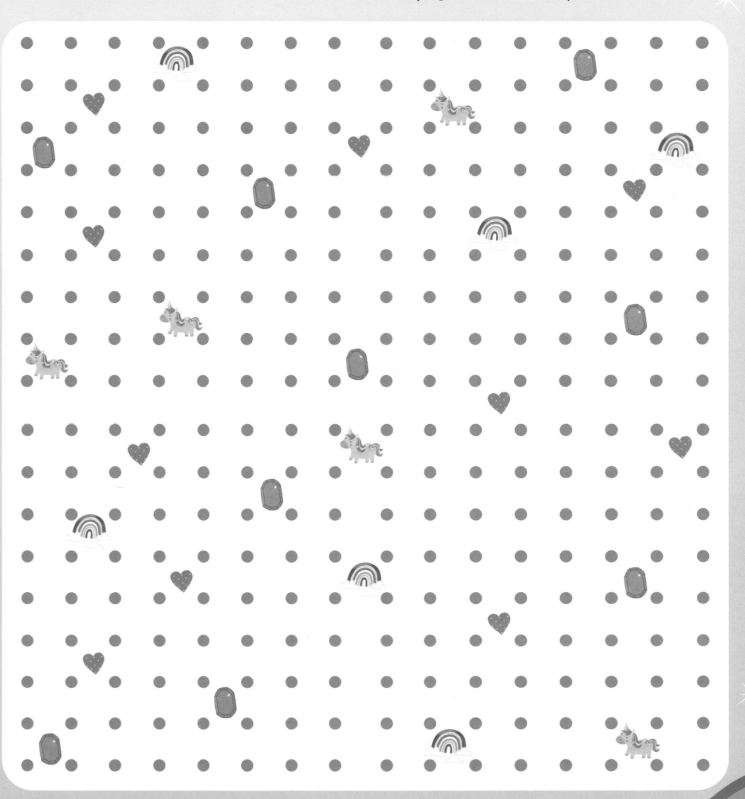

ANSWERS

Pages 8-9

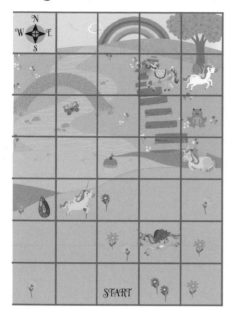

Page 10

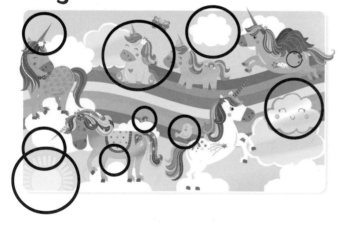

Pages 16 - 17

Page 18

Pages 20-21

Pages 22-23

1-D, 2-G, 3-B, 4-A,
5-E, 6-F, 7-C

Page 25